CAMBRIDGE
PRIMARY
MATHEMATICS

MODULE FIVE
BOOK

Roy Edwards
Mary Edwards
Alan Ward

Published by the Press Syndicate of the University of Cambridge
The Pitt Building, Trumpington Street, Cambridge CB2 1RP
40 West 20th Street, New York, NY 10011–4211, USA
10 Stamford Road, Oakleigh, Melbourne 3166, Australia

First published 1989
Eighth printing 1996

Printed in Great Britain at the University Press, Cambridge

British Library cataloguing in publication data
Edwards, Roy
Cambridge primary mathematics.
Module 5
Bk. 1
1. Mathematics
I. Title   II. Edwards, Mary   III. Ward, Alan
510
ISBN 0-521-35822-1

The authors and publishers would like to thank the many schools
and individuals who have commented on draft material for this
course. In particular, they would like to thank Anita Straker for
her contribution to the suggestions for work with computers,
Norma Anderson, Ronalyn Hargreaves ((Hyndburn Ethnic
Minority Support Service) and John Hyland Advisory Teacher
in Tameside, and the staff and pupils of Teversham C of E (A)
School.

Photographs are reproduced courtesy of:
front cover Allsport; p68 Natural History Photographic Agency

All other photographs by Graham Portlock and Justin Munro

The mathematical apparatus was kindly supplied by E J Arnold

Designed by Chris McLeod

Illustrations by Chris Ryley and Joanne Barker

Children's illustrations by Helen and Joanne Uttley, and
Lucy Bowden

Diagrams by DP Press

DP

Contents

Number 1

A

1 Draw squares like this:

odd   even   odd   even   odd

Show the pattern up to 10 squares.

2 Write the even numbers: 2, 4, 6, ☐, ☐, ☐, ☐, ☐, ☐, 20

3 Write the odd numbers: 1, 3, 5, ☐, ☐, ☐, ☐, ☐, ☐, 19

4 Use a 100 square.
Put a ring round the odd numbers.

5 Start at 31.
Write the odd numbers to 51.

6 Start at 42.
Write the even numbers to 62.

①	2	③	4	5	6
11	12	13	14	15	16
21	22	23	24	25	26
31	32	33	34	35	36
41	42	43	44	45	46
51	52	53	54	55	56

7   Which house numbers are hidden by the lorry?

8   Write all the house numbers in the row.

9   What is the middle number?

Add these pairs of odd numbers.

```
    H T U
    1 6 1
  + 1 6 3
  _____
```

Add these pairs of even numbers.

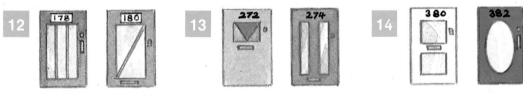

15   How many answers are even numbers?

16   How many answers are odd numbers?

Let's investigate

Write pairs of odd numbers like this. $19 + 1 = \square$
They must add up to 20.

Write pairs of even numbers which add up to 20.
Do the same for another number.

 B 123456789

Use three of these numbers each time.

H	T	U
$\square$	$\square$	$\square$

1. Make the largest odd number you can.

2. Make the largest even number.

3. Make the smallest odd number.

4. Make the smallest even number.

5. Make the number nearest to 200.

6. Make the number nearest to 222.

 250 171 292 163 344 285

7. Find which pairs of numbers add to an odd number.
   Do the sums.

8. Find which pairs of numbers add to an even number.
   Do the sums.

6

Add these pairs of numbers.
Write odd or even by each number.

9	H T U		10	H T U		11	H T U		12	H T U
	1 3 2	even		1 8 6			2 4 3			3 5 5
	+ 2 8 5	odd		+ 1 5 2			+ 1 9 4			+ 4 7 1
		odd								

These numbers are called palindromes.
They read the same forwards and backwards.

13　Write three even number palindromes.

14　Write three odd number palindromes.

Make a palindrome

Write a number　　　4 3　　　　77 is a
Write it backwards　+3 4　　　　palindrome
Add　　　　　　　　　　77

Do the same with these numbers.

15　35　　　16　13　　　17　21　　　18　62

Let's investigate Make the palindrome 99.

Write a number
Write it backwards   + □□

9 9

Find other numbers to make it.
Write other palindromes that can be made like this.

C   Draw this: Do the puzzle.

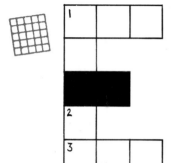

Across
1 Four hundred and thirty-two add
one hundred and ninety-one.
3 294 + 135

Down
1 The fifth even number after 53.
2 The palindrome made from 31.

Let's investigate

This is a two-step palindrome.

Write a number	5 7
Write it backwards	+ 7 5
Add	1 3 2
Write it backwards	+ 2 3 1
Add	3 6 3

363 is a palindrome.

Find other palindromes like this.

Number 2

A

1. How many campers are there?

2. Three go to get wood. How many are left?

3. Four more go to cook. How many are left?

4. Five more go to swim. How many are left?

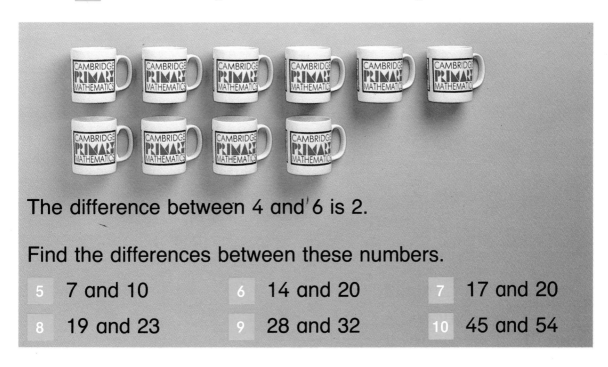

The difference between 4 and 6 is 2.

Find the differences between these numbers.

5. 7 and 10

6. 14 and 20

7. 17 and 20

8. 19 and 23

9. 28 and 32

10. 45 and 54

11 There are 150 children in the playground.
50 go inside. How many are left outside?

12 There are 242 children.
124 are girls. How many are boys?

13 There are 242 children.
115 go to camp. How many are left?

14	H T U	**15**	H T U	**16**	H T U	**17**	H T U
	3 5 6		2 3 5		4 2 3		2 7 4
	− 1 2 8		− 1 1 9		− 2 1 6		− 1 3 5

Let's investigate

Start at 100.
Count back in nines.
Write the numbers.
Find a pattern.

Start at other numbers.
Count back in nines.
Find the patterns for these.

1	2	3	4	5	6	7	8	9	10
11	12	13	14	15	16	17	18	19	20
21	22	23	24	25	26	27	28	29	30
31	32	33	34	35	36	37	38	39	40
41	42	43	44	45	46	47	48	49	50
51	52	53	54	55	56	57	58	59	60
61	62	63	64	65	66	67	68	69	70
71	72	73	74	75	76	77	78	79	80
81	82	83	84	85	86	87	88	89	90
91	92	93	94	95	96	97	98	99	100

B On a school journey the children travelled 281 miles. They wrote about it.

We went to Scotland.
It was 281 miles.
We stopped after
105 miles.

1 How many miles to go?

We played a game of "How Far to Go?"
Find how far still to go when we have
gone this far.

2 132 miles   **3** 144 miles   **4** 153 miles

We are going up the M6
I looked up the miles to
go in my map book.

Stoke 28
Preston 91
Penrith 159
Carlisle 178
Glasgow 274

5 How far is it from Penrith to Carlisle?

6 How far is it from Stoke to Preston?

7 How far is it from Penrith to Glasgow?

8 How far is it from Stoke to Glasgow?

Do these in your head. Check with a calculator.

9	42 − 19	10	42 − 29	11	42 − 39
12	74 − 19	13	74 − 29	14	74 − 39
15	85 − 19	16	85 − 29	17	85 − 39

Let's investigate

Put numbers in the boxes.

How many different subtractions can you make?

```
  H T U
  3 9 □
−   1 □ □
  ─────
  2 1 1
```

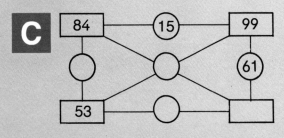

C

Along each line, the number in the circle is the difference between the numbers in the boxes.

Copy and complete the diagram.

Let's investigate

Find ways to complete this diagram.

Make up one of your own.

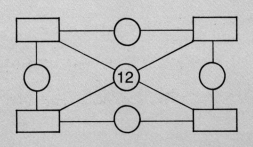

12

Shape 1

 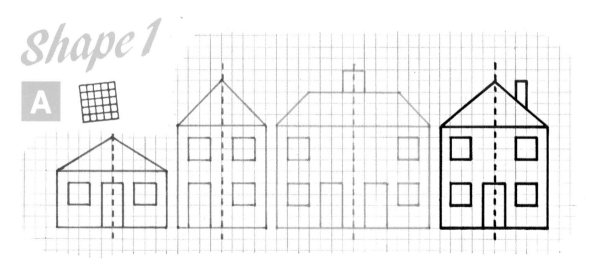

You need a mirror. Put it on each dotted line.

1 Which houses still look the same?

2 Which have symmetry?

3 Which do not have symmetry?

4 Put your mirror on the black dotted line.
Draw the house you see. Does it have symmetry?

Put your mirror on the dotted lines.

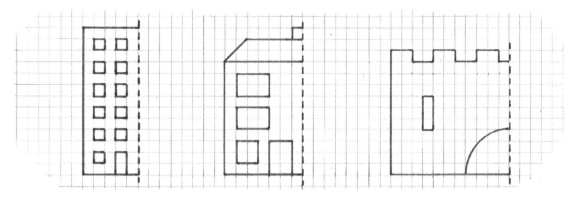

5 Draw the whole shapes.

6 Draw each line of symmetry.

7 Draw a shop which has symmetry.

Let's investigate

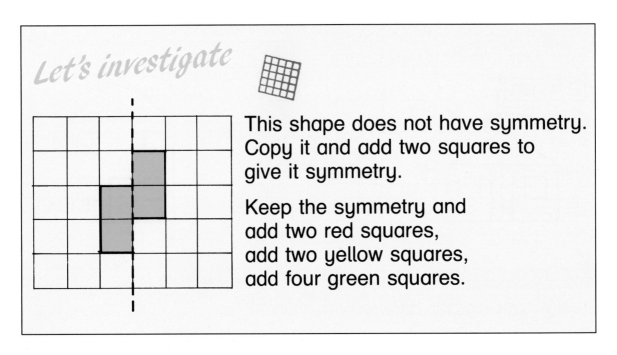

This shape does not have symmetry.
Copy it and add two squares to
give it symmetry.

Keep the symmetry and
add two red squares,
add two yellow squares,
add four green squares.

B 1 Put your mirror on each line of symmetry.
Draw the shapes you see.

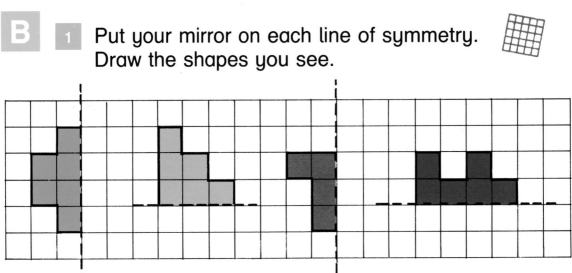

2 Which flags have symmetry?
Use your mirror to find out.

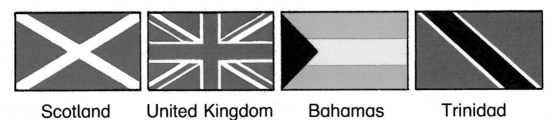

Scotland   United Kingdom   Bahamas   Trinidad

3 Copy and complete these flags.
Each flag has symmetry.

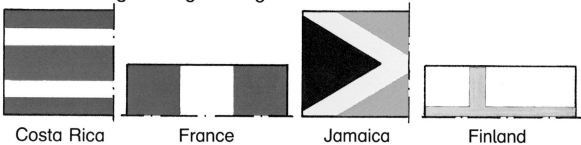

Costa Rica   France   Jamaica   Finland

Let's investigate

Design and colour flags.

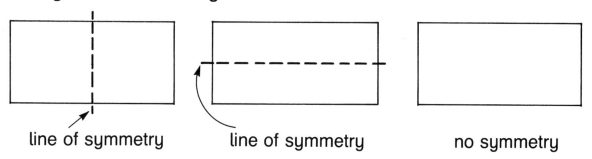

line of symmetry   line of symmetry   no symmetry

C

1 This word has symmetry.
Write some other words with symmetry.

Let's investigate

Use just one side of a mirror.

Place it so that you can see only one square.

Move it to see 2, 3, 4, 5, 6 squares.

Number 3

A

1 1 ladybird has ☐ legs.

  2 ladybirds have ☐ legs.

  3 ladybirds have ☐ legs.

2 Write the tables of 6 up to
  $10 \times 6 =$ ☐

$0 \times 6 = 0$	$6 \times 0 = 0$
$1 \times 6 = 6$	$6 \times 1 = 6$
$2 \times 6 =$ ☐	$6 \times 2 =$ ☐

3 Each lily has 6 petals.
  Copy this pattern and finish it.

lilies	petals
1	6
2	12
3	
4	
5	
6	
7	
8	
9	
10	

16

4 How many petals do 10 lilies have?

5 How many petals do 15 lilies have?

6	H T U
	2 6
×	6

7	H T U
	3 4
×	6

8	H T U
	4 2
×	6

9	H T U
	5 1
×	6

10 There are 9 flowers in each bunch.
How many flowers in 2 bunches?

11 How many flowers in 6 bunches?

12 Copy the pattern and finish it.

bunches	1	2	3	4	5	6	7	8	9	10
flowers	9									

13 Write the tables of 9 up to 10 × 9 = ☐

0 × 9 = 0	9 × 0 = 0
1 × 9 = 9	9 × 1 = 9

14	H T U	15	H T U	16	H T U	17	H T U
	1 8		3 6		2 2		4 5
	× 9		× 9		× 9		× 9
	─────		─────		─────		─────

Let's investigate

Use a 100 square.
Colour the pattern of 9.
Write, draw or talk about
the pattern.

Do the same for 6.

1	2	3	4	5	6	7	8	9	10
11	12	13	14	15	16	17	18	19	20
21	22	23	24	25	26	27	28	29	30
31	32	33	34	35	36	37	38	39	40

B

1   6   12   18 ☐ ☐ ☐ ☐ ☐ ☐ ☐

2   What do you notice about the last digit each time?

3   Carry on adding 6. Go as far as 96.
Is the pattern the same?

4   If you carried on would 123 appear in the pattern?
Why do you think this is?

5   9   18   27 ☐ ☐ ☐ ☐ ☐ ☐ ☐

6   What do you notice about the last digit
each time?

7   What other pattern can you see?

8   Draw 5 pictures to show where
you might find the number 6.

18

Find the quickest way to do these.

9   17 + 17 + 17 + 17 + 17 + 17

10   42 + 42 + 42 + 42 + 42 + 42

11   53 + 53 + 53 + 53 + 53 + 53

12   36 + 36 + 36 + 36 + 36 + 36

13
```
H T U
  6 5
×   6
─────
```

14
```
H T U
  4 9
×   6
─────
```

15
```
H T U
  7 7
×   6
─────
```

16
```
H T U
  5 4
×   6
─────
```

17   Copy and finish the table.

Pattern of 9
Add the digits

9	18	27	36	45	54	63	72	81	90
9	1 + 8 = ☐	2 + 7 = ☐							

18
```
H T U
  5 9
×   9
─────
```

19
```
H T U
  2 7
×   9
─────
```

20
```
H T U
  3 4
×   9
─────
```

21
```
H T U
  7 8
×   9
─────
```

22   Add up the digits in each answer above.
Write what you notice when you multiply by 9.

Let's investigate

Find out what happens when you multiply odd numbers.

What happens when you multiply even numbers?

What happens when you multiply odd and even numbers together?

1
$6 \times 2 = 12$
$16 \times 2 = 32$
$26 \times 2 = \square$
$36 \times 2 = \square$

Carry on to 46×2
What pattern do you notice in the answers?

2 Do the pattern for 3.
$6 \times 3 = 18$
$16 \times 3 = \square$

Carry on to 46×3.
What pattern can you see in the answers?

3 Now do the pattern for 4.
$6 \times 4 = 24$
$16 \times 4 = \square$

Carry on to 46×4.
What is the pattern in your answers?

Let's investigate

Multiply this pattern of numbers by 2.

9 19 29 39 49

Multiply the pattern by 4.

Now multiply it by 5.

What do you notice?

Does this work for other patterns of numbers?

Area 1

 A   Write the area of these numbers.

1
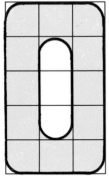

2

Count $\frac{1}{2}$ squares (or greater) as whole squares – don't count anything less than $\frac{1}{2}$ a square.

Area = ☐ squares   Area = ☐ squares

3
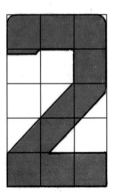

4
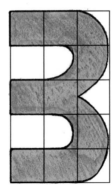

5
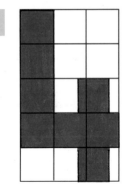

Area = ☐ squares   Area = ☐ squares   Area = ☐ squares

6   Draw two of the numbers 5, 6, 7, 8, 9, on grids like this one. Write the areas.

Let's investigate

Draw some capital letters with the same area as each other.

B Write the area of these letters.

1

Area = ☐ squares

2
Area = ☐ squares

3
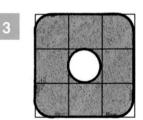
Area = ☐ squares

4 Draw the letters a, n and v on the same size of grid. Write their areas.

5
Area = ☐ squares

6
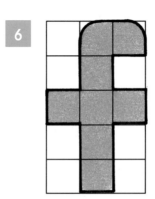
Area = ☐ squares

7
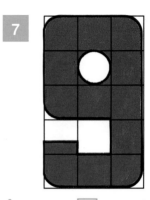
Area = ☐ squares

8 Draw the letters k and h on the same size of grid. Write their areas.

9 Draw the word four on squared paper.
Copy the letters above.
Write the area of the word four.

Let's investigate

Which letters can you draw with areas
of 10 squares each?

1 Copy and cut out these letters T and H. Write their areas.

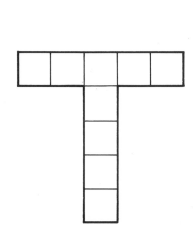 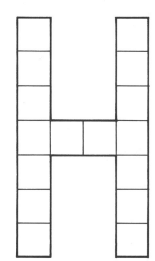

Area of T = ☐ squares   Area of H = ☐ squares

2 Cut the letter T into three pieces, and rearrange them to make a square. Draw it and write its area.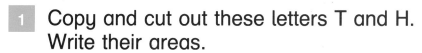

3 Cut the letter H into three pieces, and rearrange them to make another square. Draw it and write its area.

Let's investigate

What is the area of the letter L?

Draw one with all its sides twice as long. What is the area now? What do you notice?

Try this with other letters.

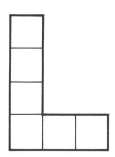

Number 4

1. How many brownies are there?

2. How many sixes are there? $18 \div 6 = \square$

3. The brownies are in 2 teams.
   How many are in each team? $18 \div 2 = \square$

1	2	3	4	5	6
7	8	9	10	11	12
13	14	15	16	17	18
19	20	21	22	23	24
25	26	27	28	29	30
31	32	33	34	35	36
37	38	39	40	41	42
43	44	45	46	47	48
49	50	51	52	53	54
55	56	57	58	59	60

$$12 \div 6 = 2$$

$$6 \overline{)12} \frac{2}{}$$

$$\frac{12}{6} = 2$$

4. $24 \div 6$

5. $48 \div 6$

6. $6 \overline{)36}$

7. $6 \overline{)60}$

8. $\dfrac{42}{6}$

9. $\dfrac{30}{6}$

24

10 $45 \div 9$

11 $72 \div 9$

12 $9\overline{)63}$

13 $9\overline{)27}$

14 $\dfrac{18}{9}$

15 $\dfrac{54}{9}$

1	2	3	4	5	6	7	8	9
10	11	12	13	14	15	16	17	18
19	20	21	22	23	24	25	26	27
28	29	30	31	32	33	34	35	36
37	38	39	40	41	42	43	44	45
46	47	48	49	50	51	52	53	54
55	56	57	58	59	60	61	62	63
64	65	66	67	68	69	70	71	72
73	74	75	76	77	78	79	80	81
82	83	84	85	86	87	88	89	90

$2\overline{)24}$

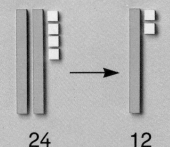

24   12   12

$2\overline{)24}^{\,12}$

16 $2\overline{)28}$

17 $2\overline{)44}$

18 $3\overline{)63}$

19 $4\overline{)84}$

20 $2\overline{)64}$

21 $4\overline{)48}$

22 $3\overline{)39}$

23 $5\overline{)55}$

24 $2\overline{)36}$

25 $2\overline{)30}$

26 $2\overline{)52}$

27 $2\overline{)54}$

Let's investigate

Put numbers in the boxes.
There must be no remainders.

$2\overline{)7\square}$ $2\overline{)\square 4}$

Find other ways to do them.

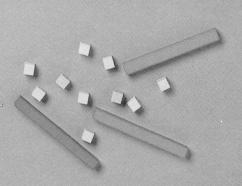

B

1. How many children are there?

2. How many lanes are there?

3. How many children are in each lane?
   $$24 \div \square = \square$$

4. If they can use only four lanes, how many will be in each?

5. Another club has twice as many children. How many would be in each of the six lanes?

6 Put 27 dancers into groups of 9. How many groups?

7 Put 27 dancers into groups of 3. How many groups?

8
$27 \div 9 = \square$ $9 \times \square = 27$
$27 \div 3 = \square$ $3 \times \square = 27$

9 $3\overline{)84}$ **10** $4\overline{)56}$ **11** $3\overline{)51}$ **12** $4\overline{)72}$

13 Copy this square. Do these and colour the answers on your square.

$12 \div 6$ $45 \div 5$ $6\overline{)18}$ $\dfrac{63}{9}$ $\dfrac{36}{6}$

2	9	3
1	7	5
4	6	8

What letter have you made?

14 Make up another number square.
Write questions to make the letter L.

Let's investigate

Use × or ÷ and these numbers.
Write as many number sentences as you can.

$\square \times \square = \square$ $\square \div \square = \square$

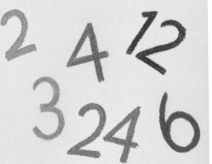

There are 36 children.

1. How many teams are there for six-a-side football?

2. How many games can they play at one time?

3. Rounders needs nine in a team.
   How many teams can play at one time?

Let's investigate

12 will divide exactly by 2, 3 and 4.

$$12 \div 2 = 6 \qquad 12 \div 3 = 4 \qquad 12 \div 4 = 3$$

Find numbers that will each divide exactly by 3, 6 and 9.

Find numbers that will each divide exactly by 2, 3 and 5.

Data 1

A

Class 4's new books

Graph of new books

number of books

class 1   class 2   class 3   class 4

1   How many new books are in class 4?

2   Draw the graph for the four classes.

3   How many new books are in class 3?

4   How many new books are in class 2?

5   Class 2 have twice as many as class ☐

6   Class 4 have half as many as class ☐

7   Put the classes in the order of
    the new books they have.
    Start with the class with most books.
    Draw a graph like this to show them.

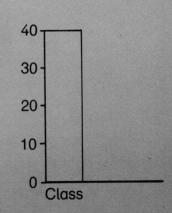

40

30

20

10

0
Class

The chart shows the books the children are reading.

	with pictures	without pictures
story	Brian	Ann
not a story	Susan Tom	

8 Who is reading a story book with pictures?

9 Who is reading a story book without pictures?

10 Who are reading picture books that are not stories?

Let's investigate

Write the names of some books from your class library to fit the chart.

	with pictures	without pictures
stories		
not stories		

Write some questions for the chart.

B

	with pictures	without pictures
animals	John Sarah Andrew	Bill
no animals	Peter Rachel	Kim

1 How many children are reading picture books about animals?

2 Which girl is reading a picture book not about animals?

3 What is Bill reading?

4 Which children are not reading picture books?

30

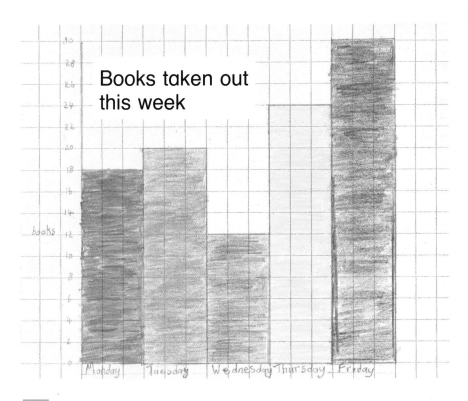

Books taken out this week

5 When were most books taken out?

6 Why do you think this was?

7 When were fewest books taken out?

8 Copy this table. Put in the numbers from the graph.

	Monday	Tuesday	Wednesday	Thursday	Friday
books					

9 These are the numbers of books taken out last week.

	Monday	Tuesday	Wednesday	Thursday	Friday
books	19	22	17	20	26

Draw the graph to show these numbers.

10 When do you think most books will be taken out next week? Why?

Let's investigate

Finish this graph.
Give it a title and labels.

Make up some questions about your graph.

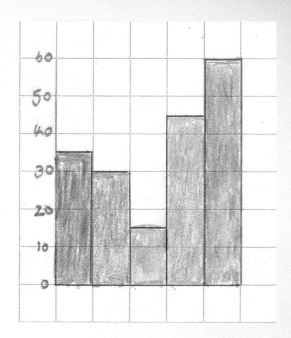

C

1 Choose 4 books from the library.
Draw a graph to show the numbers
of pages in each of the 4 books.

Let's investigate

Draw two graphs to show different
things about these books.

32

Money 1

1

	£
Mum's meal cost	2·25
Ann's meal cost	1·57
The total	

Here are some more bills. Add them up.

2 £	**3** £	**4** £	**5** £
3·46	2·48	4·74	3·56
3·26	4·71	2·72	4·27

6 Ann buys a puzzle book.

	£
She has	2·31
The book costs	1·16
The money left is	

7 What coins can Ann have left? Draw them.

8 What different coins can she have left? Draw them.

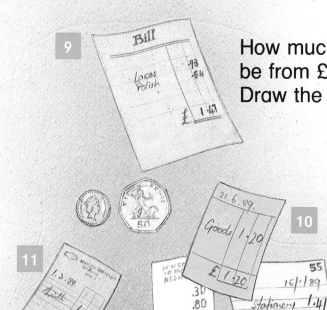

9 How much change will there be from £1·50? Draw the coins.

10 Here are some more bills. What is the change each time from £1·50? Draw the coins.

11

12

13

14 Each bag has £1 in it. How many coins are in each bag?

Let's investigate

What amounts can you make with 3 different coins? Draw them.

B

1 Each bag above has £5 in it. How many coins are in each bag?

2 Add up the bill.

3 Dad pays the bill with £4·50.
What is his change?

4 Draw the coins he can get in
the change.

HAPPY EATER
FAMILY RESTAURANTS

STARTERS	£	
MEALS	1·	51
	1·	54
SWEETS	1·	33
BEVERAGES		

5 Dad pays £3·50 for three ice creams.
He gets 10p change.
Which ones did he buy?

LARGE £1·60
MEDIUM £1·25
SMALL £0·90

6 Which other ice creams can Dad buy for £3·50?
He must buy three each time.
What will his change be for each bill?

These three things have different prices.
Each one costs more than 50p.
You must buy all three of them for
exactly £1·75.
Find different ways to price them.

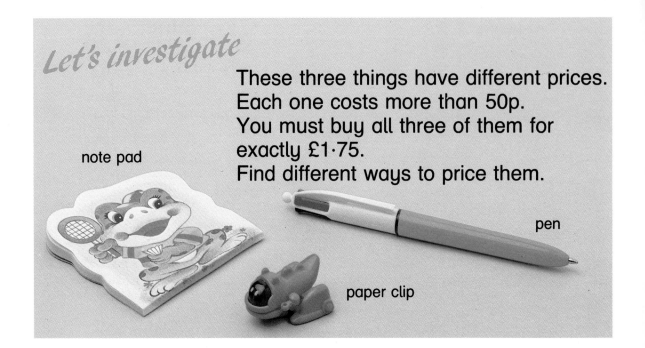

note pad

pen

paper clip

C

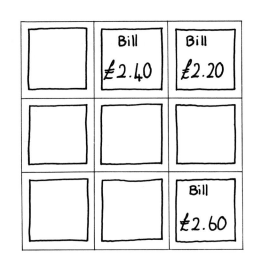

1 Each line of the magic square
adds up to £6·00.
What are the missing bills?

2 Take £1 off each bill.
Draw the new square.
Is it still a magic square?

Try to make all the amounts from £1·20 to £1·30
using 4 coins each time.
Are there any amounts you cannot make?

Try to make all the amounts using
5 coins each time.

36

Number 5

half + half = 1 whole
2 halves = 1 whole
$\frac{1}{2} + \frac{1}{2} = \frac{2}{2} = 1$

1 $1 = \dfrac{\Box}{2} = \Box$ halves

2 $\dfrac{1}{4} + \dfrac{1}{4} + \dfrac{1}{4} + \dfrac{1}{4} = \dfrac{4}{4} = 1$

$1 = \dfrac{\Box}{4}$

3 $\dfrac{1}{2} = \dfrac{\Box}{4}$ **4** $\dfrac{2}{4} = \dfrac{\Box}{2}$

5 $\dfrac{1}{4} + \dfrac{1}{4} + \dfrac{1}{4} = \dfrac{\Box}{4}$

6 $\dfrac{2}{4} + \dfrac{1}{4} = \dfrac{\Box}{\Box}$ **7** $\dfrac{1}{2} + \dfrac{1}{4} = \dfrac{\Box}{\Box}$

Let's investigate

Colour some pizza shapes to show $\frac{1}{2}$ in different ways.
Now colour some pizza shapes to show $\frac{3}{4}$ in different ways.

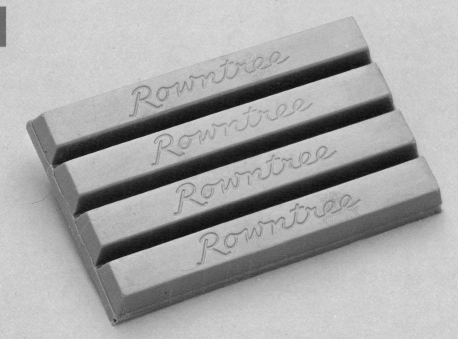

Write number sentences for these.

1 $\dfrac{3}{4} + \dfrac{1}{4} = \square$

2 $\dfrac{1}{2} + \dfrac{1}{2} = \square$

3 $\dfrac{1}{4} + \dfrac{3}{4} = \square$

4 Write different number sentences to make $\dfrac{3}{4}$.

5 Draw these. Colour $\dfrac{1}{4} + \dfrac{3}{4}$ in different ways.

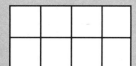

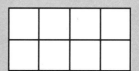

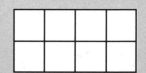

6 Draw three more rectangles like these.
Colour them to show $\dfrac{1}{2} + \dfrac{1}{2}$ in different ways.

7 Draw four more rectangles.
Show $\dfrac{1}{4} + \dfrac{1}{4} + \dfrac{1}{4} + \dfrac{1}{4}$ in different ways.

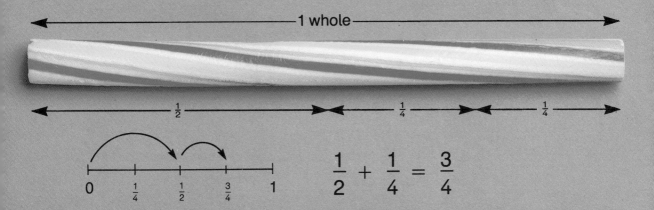

1 whole

$\frac{1}{2}$ $\frac{1}{4}$ $\frac{1}{4}$

$$\frac{1}{2} + \frac{1}{4} = \frac{3}{4}$$

0    $\frac{1}{4}$ $\frac{1}{2}$ $\frac{3}{4}$ 1

Write number sentences for these lines.

8

0    $\frac{1}{4}$ $\frac{1}{2}$ $\frac{3}{4}$ 1

9

0    $\frac{1}{4}$ $\frac{1}{2}$ $\frac{3}{4}$ 1

10

0    $\frac{1}{4}$ $\frac{1}{2}$ $\frac{3}{4}$ 1

11

0    $\frac{1}{4}$ $\frac{1}{2}$ $\frac{3}{4}$ 1

Let's investigate

Make up number sentences with fractions.
Draw a picture for each one.

C *Let's investigate*

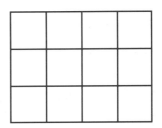

Draw rectangles like this.
Colour them in different ways,
$\frac{1}{2}$ red, $\frac{1}{4}$ blue, $\frac{1}{4}$ green.
The rectangles must have symmetry.

Length 1

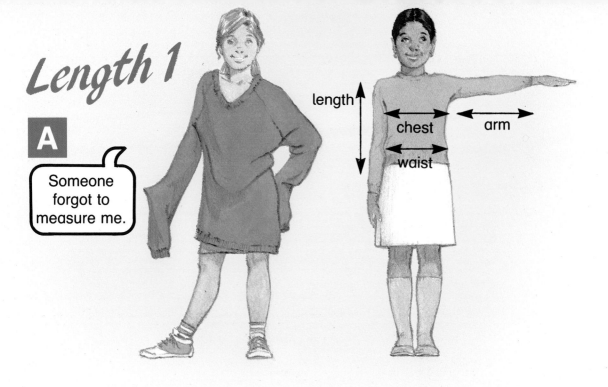

A

Someone forgot to measure me.

Find your measurements.

1. My arm is ☐ cm.

2. My chest is ☐ cm.

3. My waist is ☐ cm.

4. My jumper length is ☐ cm.

5. Work with a friend.

   Estimate a length of 2 m.

   Measure your estimate to the nearest metre.

   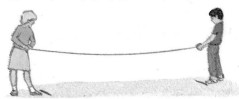

   My estimate was ☐ m.

Write these to the nearest metre.

6.

7.

8.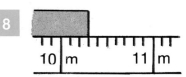

9 Draw lines the same lengths as each of your fingers.

Thumb _____ ☐ cm.

10 Which is your shortest finger?

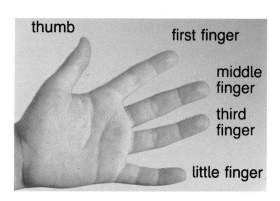

thumb
first finger
middle finger
third finger
little finger

Let's investigate

Choose some clothes.
Write your measurements to have them made.

B

1 How high can you reach? Keep your feet on the ground.

I can reach ☐ cm.

2 How high can you reach with a jump?

I can reach ☐ cm with a jump.

3 My height is ☐ cm.

4 How much higher than your height can you reach with a jump?

5 Use a tape measure or a trundle wheel.
How many metres long is your classroom?

6 A football pitch is about 100 metres long.
About how many classrooms like yours would stretch from goal to goal?

Let's investigate

Measure the left feet of some friends without their shoes on.

Ask them their shoe sizes.

Write what you notice about feet lengths and shoe sizes.

C

1 Do a long jump starting with a run.
Measure it.

2 Do a long jump starting with feet together.
Measure it.

3 Which is the longer jump?
How much further is it?

Let's investigate

Can you fit a 50 metre race in your playground?
Ask your teacher if you may mark out a track.

Can you mark out a 100 metre track?
The tracks need not be straight lines.

Weight 1

A

Easy Pizza
Flour 140g
Margarine 35g
¼ teaspoon sa...
milk to mix

Topping:
Tomato He...
Cheese to taste.

Chocolate Krispie Cake
Chocolate 125g
Krispies 45g
Melt chocolate
in bowl over hot
water.
Add crispies
and mix.

Cheese Bread Rolls
Bread Mix 283g
Cheese 175g

...d hot water
...packet
...ese P.T.O.

Find the weights.

1

	g
chocolate	125
krispies +	45
Total weight	

2

	g
flour	140
margarine +	35
Total weight	

3

	g
bread mix	283
cheese +	175
Total weight	

4 45 g of krispies are used. What weight is left?

5
$$\begin{array}{r} g \\ 246 \\ +\ 338 \\ \hline \end{array}$$

6
$$\begin{array}{r} g \\ 374 \\ +\ 165 \\ \hline \end{array}$$

7
$$\begin{array}{r} g \\ 462 \\ -\ 239 \\ \hline \end{array}$$

8
$$\begin{array}{r} g \\ 394 \\ -\ 186 \\ \hline \end{array}$$

9 Write the answers in order.
Start with the lightest.

Let's investigate

Estimate 200 g of cubes.
Put them in a bag.
Weigh them to see if you were right.

Do the same with 50 g, 100 g, 500 g, of cubes.

B

Apple pie
Flour   170g
Margarine 85g
Apples   500g

Blackberry pie
Flour   170g
Margarine   85g
Blackberries 450g

Gooseberry pie
Flour   170g
Margarine   85g
Gooseberries 430g

1 What is the weight of each pie before cooking?

2

Nut cookies
150g Butter
100g Sugar
200g Flour
50g Nuts

Cherry shortbread
125g Flour
25g Cornflour
50g Sugar
100g Butter
25g Cherries

Chocolate biscuits
100g Butter
100g Sugar
150g Flour
2 Eggs
100g Chocolate buttons

How much of each item will you
need to make all three recipes?

butter ☐ g   chocolate ☐ g   eggs ☐
sugar ☐ g   cornflour ☐ g   nuts ☐ g
flour ☐ g   cherries ☐ g

3 How many packets of each grocery do you need to make all three recipes?

4 How much of each will be left over?

Let's investigate

The pie weighs 655 g.
After 3 pieces are eaten it weighs 345 g.
What can the 3 pieces each weigh?
Find different answers.

C

	Total weight	Weight of tin or jar	Weight of contents
1 Peaches	☐ g	59 g	416 g
2 Soup	490 g	65 g	☐ g
3 Jam	480 g	☐ g	273 g

Let's investigate

Write the recipe for 5 people.
Now do it again for more people.

Syrup tart for 2
66 g pastry
100 g syrup
16 g breadcrumbs

Capacity 1

1000 millilitres = 1 litre
1000 ml = 1 l

1 How many ml of water are in the jug?

2 $\frac{1}{2}$ l of lemonade = ☐ ml.

You need a cup, a yogurt pot and a mug.

3 Estimate which of them will hold a can of lemon and lime.

4 Measure how many ml each one holds.

5 Which of them holds more than 250 ml? Were you right?

How many ml in these?

6 1 can of cola and 1 can of lemonade.

7 1 can of cola and 1 can of lemon and lime.

8 How many cans of lemon and lime make up $\frac{1}{2}$ l?

Fruit punch recipe

Orange	300ml
Apple	160ml
Pineapple	140ml
Lemonade	380ml

Find the difference in ml between these drinks.

9   1 bottle of orange and 1 bottle of pineapple.

10   1 can of cola and 1 can of lemonade.

11   1 can of lemon and lime and 1 bottle of pineapple.

Let's investigate

How could you make a large ice cream tub hold only
a litre of water?
Where would you make a hole?
Why would you make it there?

B

1   How many ml are in the fruit punch?

2   How much is left after 2 glassfuls?

3   How much is left after 6 glassfuls?

4   How much is left after 8 glassfuls?

120 ml

A larger glass holds 200 ml.

5 How many large glasses can be filled with the punch?

6 How much is left over?

7 Write out the recipe making each ingredient 20 ml less.

8 How many ml of punch does it make now?

Recipe for
fruit punch

Orange	300ml
Apple	100ml
Pineapple	140 ml
Lemonade	380ml

Let's investigate

Use the same ingredients.
Write some recipes for $\frac{1}{2}$ litre of punch.

C

Each drink is 250 ml.
It is made with 50 ml of orange squash. The rest is water.

1 How many drinks can be made from 1 l of orange squash?

2 How many litres of water would you need for 10 drinks?

Let's investigate

How many bottles of squash would make drinks for all your class?
How much squash would be left?

Time 1

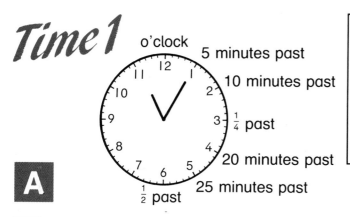

o'clock
5 minutes past
10 minutes past
$\frac{1}{4}$ past
20 minutes past
25 minutes past
$\frac{1}{2}$ past

In 1829 George Stephenson's steam engine, called the Rocket, travelled at a speed of 29 mph. People were amazed because this was faster than a horse could gallop.

A

1 Copy the clock.
The time is ☐ minutes past 11.

Write the times.

2   **3**    **4**   **5**

Show these times on clock faces.

6 | half past 8 | **7** | 5 minutes past 4 | **8** | 10 minutes past 2 |

9 The next train leaves at 11.05. This is ☐ past ☐.

10 Show the departure times on clock faces.

Departures

Liverpool	9:15
Blackpool	9:25
Glasgow	10:10
Preston	10:30
Manchester	11:00

49

In the 1950s diesel and electric trains began to be used. The diesel engine was invented by Rudolf Diesel, a German engineer.

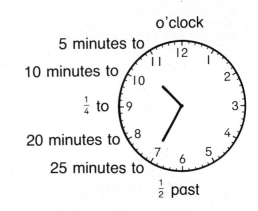

o'clock
5 minutes to
10 minutes to
$\frac{1}{4}$ to
20 minutes to
25 minutes to
$\frac{1}{2}$ past

11 Copy the clock.
The time is ☐ to 11

Write the times.

12    **13**    **14**    **15**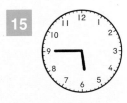

The next arrival will be 10:35.

16 It is 35 minutes past 10 or ☐ to 11.

17 Show the arrival times below on clock faces.

Let's investigate

Think of other places when we need to know the time.
What things tell us the time?

Arrivals	
Bristol	10:35
London	10:40
Cambridge	11:50
Bath	12:55

HARBURY

IV 03

B Show each of the times in these two ways.

1 quarter past 1 **2** quarter to 6 **3** 10 o'clock

`2:20`

4 5 past 2 **5** 20 to 12 **6** 5 to 3

7 Start at `4:25` → `   :   ` →

Keep adding 10 minutes until you reach `5:35`

Let's investigate

Use : and 5 and 0 as many times
as you wish.
Make different digital times.
Write them in order.

5 minutes

C Show these
in two ways.

1 50 minutes **2** 35 minutes

3 45 minutes **4** 55 minutes

Let's investigate

Write pairs of digital
times.
They must show
a difference of
25 minutes.
The hour numbers
must be different.

Now British Rail
runs more trains at
100 mph during their
journey than any other
railway in the world.

Angles 1

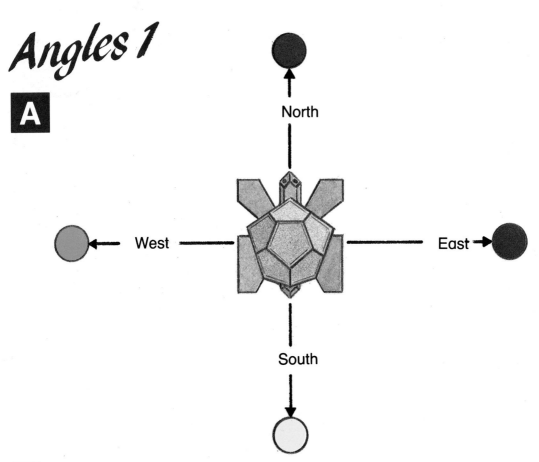

North

West ← ← → East

South

1 The turtle turns to Blue. It faces ——— .

2 The turtle turns to Red. It faces ——— .

3 The turtle turns to Yellow. It faces ——— .

4 The turtle turns to Green. It faces ——— .

A square corner is a right-angle.
A right-angle is 90°.

	5	6	7	8	9	10
Turtle faces	N	N	S	E	W	S	E
It turns clockwise	90°	180°	90°	180°	90°	180°	90°
It now faces	E						

52

Let's investigate

How can you walk
from home to school
on this map?
One way is shown.

Write other ways to get
from home to school.
Show the directions.

Home →

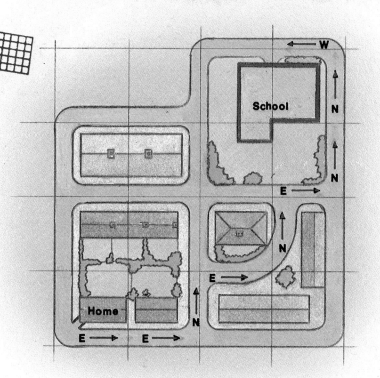

 B

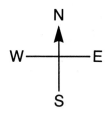

1

Copy this plan.
Name the buildings.

The post office (P.O.) is
N from Tom's house.

The shop is W from the P.O.

The school is W from
the house.

The church (⚲) is S of
the school.

The telephone (T) is E
of the house.

2 Put some more buildings on the plan.
Give directions to find them.

3 Look at the directions for the house. Draw and write directions for the school.

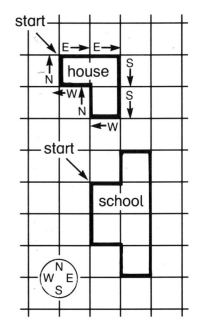

4 Draw a shop using these directions.
N → E → E → E → S → S →
W → N → W → W

Let's investigate

Draw some plans of your own.
Give the directions.

C

1 Use a map of your area.
Write places that are to the north, south, east and west of you.
Show them on a plan.

Let's investigate

Use a world map.
Find countries that are to the north, south, east and west of you.

Choose another country.
Find places that are north, south, east and west of it.

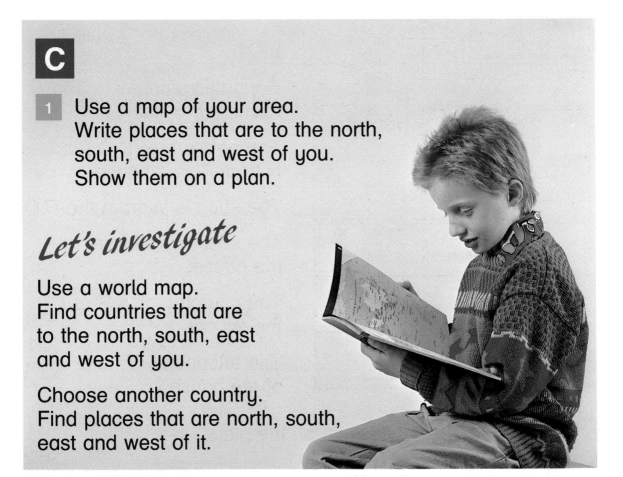

Number 6

A

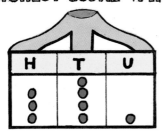

ROLLERBALL

8 BALLS EACH GO
HIGHEST SCORE WINS

H	T	U

NUMBER SPIN

TWO SPINS
SCORE 500 OR MORE
TO WIN

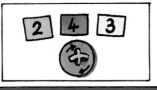

Draw the roller balls
for these scores.

1. Tara 300 + 40 + 1 = ☐
2. Suzy 400 + 10 + 3 = ☐
3. David 200 + 50 + 1 = ☐
4. Saeed 300 + 30 + 2 = ☐
5. Who won the Rollerball?

Add up the scores for
Number Spin.

6. Suzy
   127
   267

7. David
   349
   172

8. Saeed
   221
   278

9. Tara
   243
   156

10. Who won the
    Number Spin?

55

Add the scores.

11 Suzy   115   163

12 Tara   129   182

13 Saeed 106   126

14 David 113   136

15 Who won the Lucky Dip?

FIND THE NUMBERS

Write the patterns to win!

16

| 15 →20→ ? → ? |
| 10 ↑ +5 ? |
| 5   ? |

17

36 +10

18

42 +9

Let's investigate

Make up your own 'Find the numbers'.
You must end on 120.

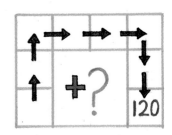

+?   120

B WHEEL OF FORTUNE

1. Add the numbers for each colour.

2. Highest score wins. Which colour wins?

3. What is the highest possible score?

NUMBER HUNT

Find the numbers marked [?] Two odd numbers win.

4

→ + 10

↓
14	24	
?		
		?

+ 2

5

→ + 10

↓
35		
	?	
		?

+ 3

6

→ + 20

↓
25		
?		
?		

+ 3

7

→ + 20

↓
37		
	?	?

+ 5

8 Which one wins?

JACKPOT

5 3 4

All three
the same
to win

Write these numbers.

9 800 + 70 + 6

10 50 + 600 + 7

11 900 + 5 + 70

12 two + three hundred + sixty

13 four + forty + four hundred

14 nine hundred + seventy + eight

15 Which one wins the jackpot?

Let's investigate

Write the numbers
of the ducks you need
to make 120.

Catch 3 ducks
       4 ducks
       5 ducks
       6 ducks

Find other ways
of winning.

The first fairs were markets.
People bought and sold goods
at them. In the Middle Ages,
people like jugglers and acrobats
used to entertain the crowds.

NUMBER SEARCH
FIND THREE NUMBER PATTERNS TO WIN

55	9	10	23	26
45	8	7	20	17
35	12	6	18	14
25	15	**5**	8	11

Find three number patterns for each of these.

1

92	86	100	92	85
98	80	90	80	78
68	74	60	70	71
62	56	**50**	57	64

2

625	725	145	149	188
525	137	141	170	179
425	133	129	161	152
325	225	**125**	134	143

Let's investigate

Make up number patterns of your own.

		15		

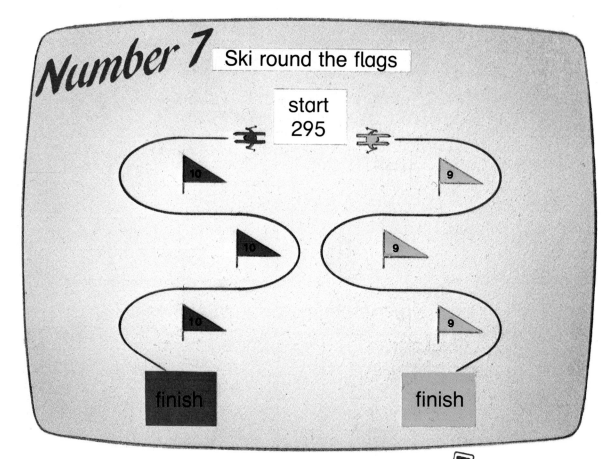

Number 7

Ski round the flags

start
295

A Subtract each number the skier passes.

1 Red
| start 295 | −10 | 285 | −10 | 275 | −10 | finish |

2 Blue
| start 295 | −9 | □ | −9 | □ | −9 | finish |

Find the finishing score for these starting numbers.

3 Red   264 → □ → □ → □

4 Blue 264 → □ → □ → □

5 Red   382 → □ → □ → □

6 Blue 382 → □ → □ → □

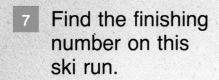

7 Find the finishing number on this ski run.

$$\begin{array}{r} 2\ 5\ 4 \\ -\quad 3\ 5 \\ \hline \end{array}$$

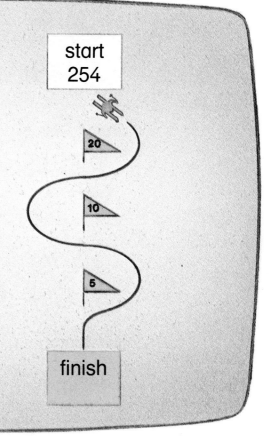

start
254

20

10

5

finish

Find the finishing number on the yellow ski run for these starting numbers.

8 start 142

9 start 381

10 start 416

11 start 628

12
$$\begin{array}{r} 2\ 6\ 3 \\ -\quad 8\ 2 \\ \hline \end{array}$$

13
$$\begin{array}{r} 3\ 2\ 7 \\ -\ 1\ 9\ 4 \\ \hline \end{array}$$

14
$$\begin{array}{r} 5\ 3\ 6 \\ -\ 2\ 5\ 4 \\ \hline \end{array}$$

Let's investigate

Use these to design a ski run of your own. Find different ways of numbering the 3 flags.

start 243

finish 220

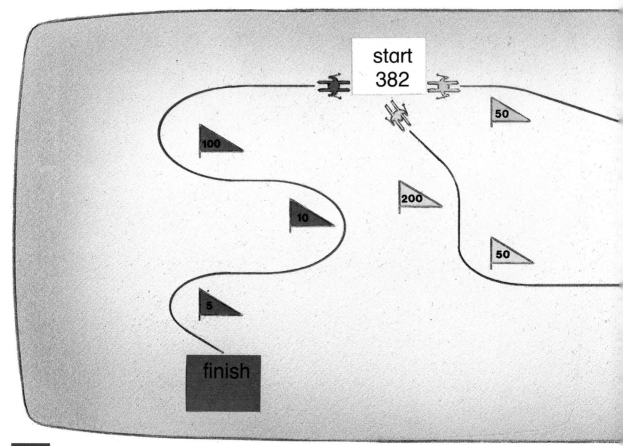

B Find the numbers at the finish of the red
ski run for these starting numbers.

1
start
382
$\xrightarrow{-100}$ ☐ $\xrightarrow{-10}$ ☐ $\xrightarrow{-5}$ ☐

2
start
472

3
start
683

4
start
257

5
start
648

Find the finishing numbers on the yellow
ski run for these starting numbers.

6
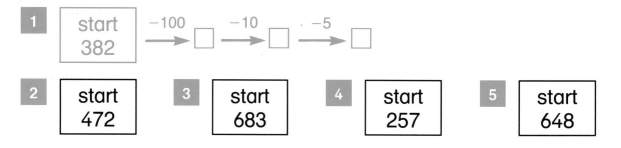
```
  3 8 2
- 2 5 6
_____
```

7 526

8 449

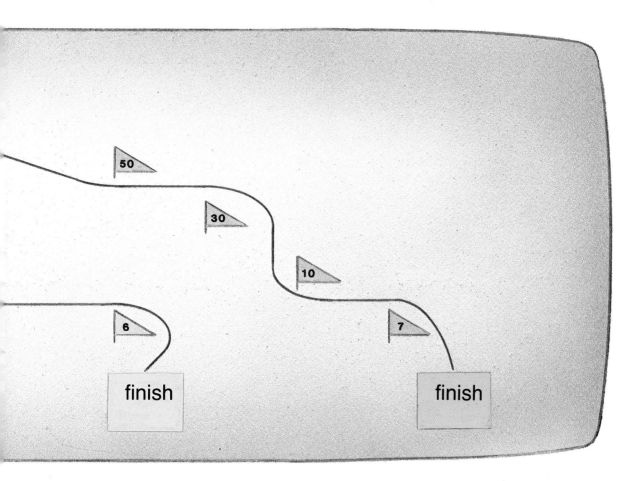

Find the finishing numbers on the blue ski run
for these starting numbers.

9  $\begin{array}{r} 3\ 8\ 2 \\ -\ 1\ 4\ 7 \\ \hline \end{array}$

10 629   **11** 537

Let's investigate

Find different scores for the
starting and finishing numbers.
Both numbers must be
between 100 and 299.

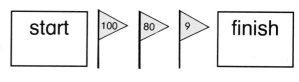

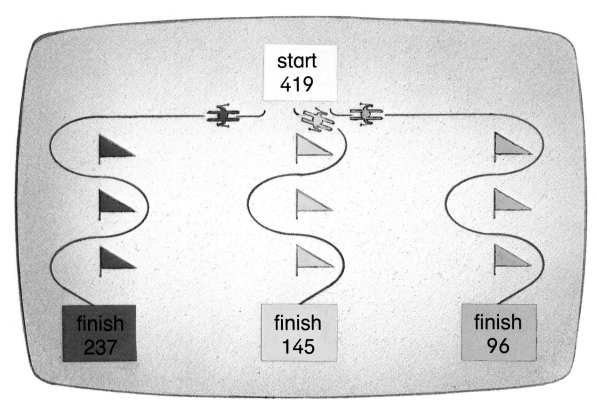

start
419

finish
237

finish
145

finish
96

 C

Find the total scores of the flags on each ski run.
Write what they could be.

1 red total = ☐

2 yellow total = ☐

3 blue total = ☐

Let's investigate

These 3 flags have odd
numbers. Which different
numbers could they be?

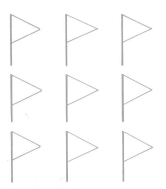

start
191

finish
124

Shape 2

A

When shapes tessellate
they leave no gaps.

1 Draw 24 squares.
   Try to make them tessellate.

   Colour the squares.

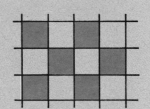

2 Do squares tessellate?

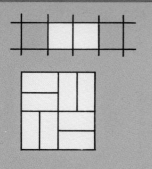

3 Draw 12 circles.
   Try to make them tessellate.

4 Do circles tessellate?

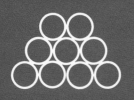

Let's investigate

Draw a rectangle like this.

Draw more of these rectangles
to make a tessellation.
Make different tessellations
with rectangles.

1 Draw round some equilateral triangles. Try to make them tessellate.

2 Draw round some hexagons. Try to make them tessellate.

3 Draw round some pentagons. Try to make them tessellate.

4 Which of the shapes tessellate?

5 Which of the shapes in the patchworks will tessellate?

Cut out 8 equilateral triangles all the same size.

Fit them together to make a four-sided shape.
Draw them.

Make shapes with more than four sides.

C 1 Cut out some equilateral triangles all the same size.

How many do you need to make a hexagon?

Let's investigate

Choose two shapes.
Make a tessellation using
them both.

Can you find other shapes
that tessellate together?

Draw the tessellations.

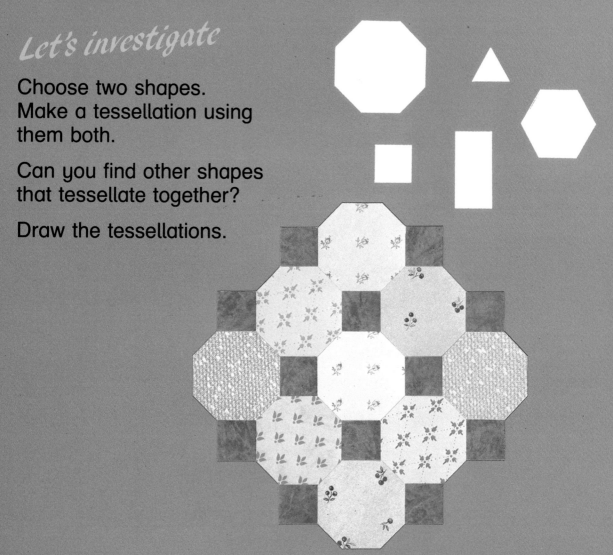

Number 8

A

1 One spider has ☐ legs.

2 Two spiders have ☐ legs.

3 Three spiders have ☐ legs.

Write the tables of 8 up to $10 \times 8 = $ ☐ .

4
$0 \times 8 = 0$
$1 \times 8 = 8$
$2 \times 8 = 16$
$3 \times 8 = $ ☐
$4 \times 8 = $ ☐
$5 \times 8 = $
6×8

5
$8 \times 0 = 0$
$8 \times 1 = 8$
$8 \times 2 = 16$
$8 \times 3 = $ ☐
$8 \times 4 = $ ☐
$= $ ☐

How many legs do these have?

6 11 spiders   **7** 12 spiders   **8** 13 spiders   **9** 14 spiders

10
$$\begin{array}{r} 3\,2 \\ \times\ \ 8 \\ \hline \end{array}$$

11
$$\begin{array}{r} 2\,4 \\ \times\ \ 8 \\ \hline \end{array}$$

12
$$\begin{array}{r} 4\,6 \\ \times\ \ 8 \\ \hline \end{array}$$

13
$$\begin{array}{r} 5\,3 \\ \times\ \ 8 \\ \hline \end{array}$$

14 Write the tables of 7 up to 10 × 7 = ☐ .

$0 \times 7 = 0$
$1 \times 7 = 7$
$2 \times 7 =$

$7 \times 0 = 0$
$7 \times 1 = 7$
$\times 2 = 14$

15 How many days in 1 week?

16 How many days in 3 weeks?

17 Gill's baby sister is 14 weeks old.
How many days old is the baby?

How many days old
are these babies?

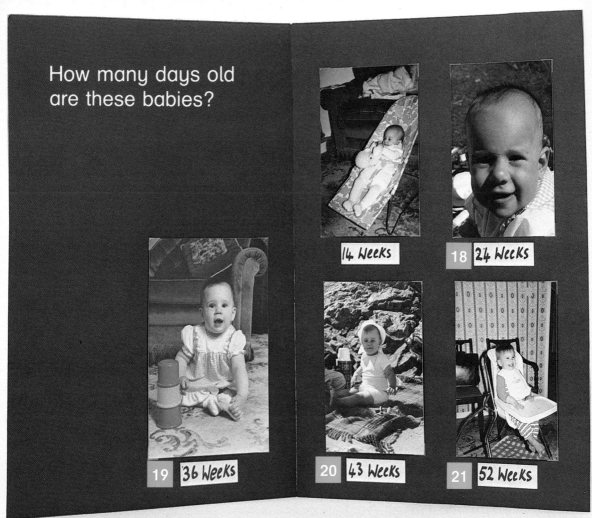

14 Weeks

18 24 Weeks

19 36 Weeks

20 43 Weeks

21 52 Weeks

1 child has 10 toes.

22 2 children have ☐ toes.

23 3 children have ☐ toes.

24 Copy this table and finish it.

1	2	3	4	5	6	7	8	9	10
10	20	30							

25 What do you notice about the answers?

26 14 children are paddling.
How many toes are in the water?

27 12 × 10   **28** 17 × 10   **29** 15 × 10   **30** 13 × 10

Let's investigate

What is the pattern here?   3 6 9 12 15 18 21 24

Multiply each number by 10.
What is the pattern now?

What do you notice?
Does it work for other patterns?

B

1 | 7 shelves
23 books on each

How many books?

2 | 8 shelves
19 books on each

How many books?

3 ☐ × 7 = 35   **4** 8 × ☐ = 56   **5** ☐ × 8 = 64

6 4 × ☐ = 28   **7** ☐ × 7 = 49   **8** 9 × ☐ = 72

9 ☐ × 8 = 40   **10** 6 × 7 = ☐   **11** ☐ × 8 = 48

12 10 × ☐ = 80   **13** 7 × ☐ = 63   **14** ☐ × 4 = 32

15 Which number is in both the tables of 7 and 8?

$$3 \xrightarrow{\times 10} 30 \xrightarrow{\times 10} 300$$

16 $4 \xrightarrow{\times 10} \square \xrightarrow{\times 10} \square$

17 $\square \xrightarrow{\times 10} \square \xrightarrow{\times 10} 900$

18 $\square \xrightarrow{\times 10} 10 \xrightarrow{\times 10} \square$

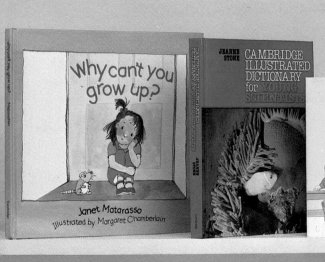
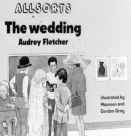

71

Work these out in the easiest way.

19 $5 \times 7 \times 2 = \square$ **20** $2 \times 5 \times 6 = \square$ **21** $8 \times 2 \times 5 = \square$

22 $2 \times 9 \times 5 = \square$ **23** $7 \times 5 \times 2 = \square$ **24** $5 \times 5 \times 2 = \square$

Let's investigate

Choose four numbers that follow each other 1 2 3 4	Write them like this and multiply	$2 \times 3 = 6$ $1 \times 4 = 4$ Difference 2

Try this with other numbers that follow each other.
What do you notice?

C

1 Find the missing number on the machine.

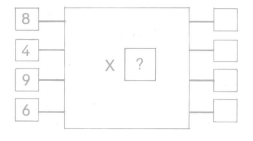

Put in the other numbers.

28   63
56
42

Let's investigate

Look at this machine.

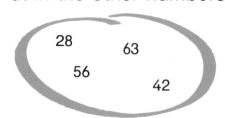

INPUT → MACHINE $\times 8 + \square$ → OUTPUT odd number

Put numbers in the boxes to make it work.
What do you notice?

Try this machine.

INPUT → MACHINE $\times 7 + \square$ → OUTPUT odd number

What do you notice this time?

Area 2

A

This is 1 cm².
Each side of the
square is 1 cm long.

Find the area of
each colour.

1 Red   ☐ cm²

2 Blue   ☐ cm²

3 Green   ☐ cm²

4 Yellow   ☐ cm²

5 What is the
   total area?

Let's investigate

Colour a patchwork cushion for the cat.

Use a rectangle of 24 squares.
Draw a pattern that has 8 red squares,
8 yellow and 8 green.
Use some half squares.

Colour a different cushion with
the same area of colours.

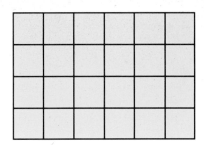

B

1. What colours have been used?

2. What is the area of each colour?

3. What is the total area of material?

4. Which colour has the greatest area?

Let's investigate

Make a picture using about 70 cm².
Choose your own colours.
What is the area of each colour?

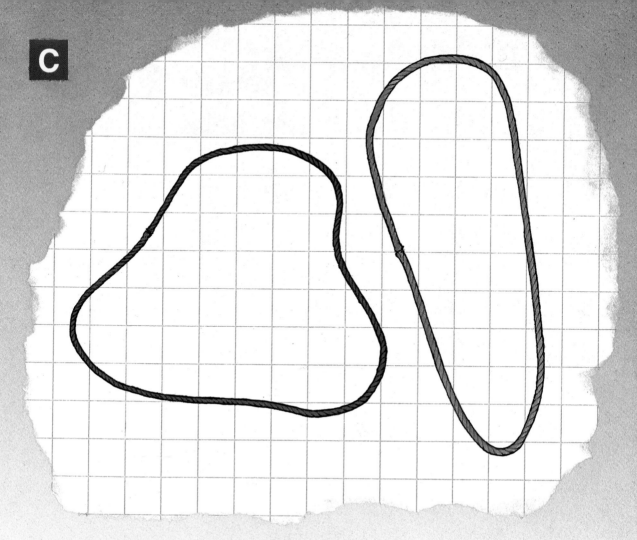

C

These shapes are made with string.
Each string is 25 cm long.

1 What is the area of each?

2 Cut a piece of string 25 cm long.
Stick it on squared paper to make a shape.
What is its area?

Let's investigate

Cut some more pieces of string 25 cm long.
Make shapes on squared paper.
What is the greatest area you can make
with one piece of string?

Number 9

A

Each player in this game has 7 cards.

1. If there are 28 cards how many children can play?

2. If there are 21 cards how many children are playing?

> Card games have been played for more than 600 years. Over 1000 card games have been invented.

1	2	3	4	5	6	7
8	9	10	11	12	13	14
15	16	17	18	19	20	21
22	23	24	25	26	27	28
29	30	31	32	33	34	35
36	37	38	39	40	41	42
43	44	45	46	47	48	49
50	51	52	53	54	55	56
57	58	59	60	61	62	63
64	65	66	67	68	69	70

3. How many 7s in 35?

4. How many 7s in 21?

5. How many 7s in 7?

6. How many 7s in 63?

7. How many 7s in 49?

8. How many 7s in 70?

9. $7\overline{)14}$

10. $7\overline{)28}$

11. $7\overline{)56}$

12. $7\overline{)42}$

13. $21 \div 7$

14. $63 \div 7$

15. $35 \div 7$

16. $49 \div 7$

In this game each player has
8 cards.

17 If there are 32 cards
how many children can play?

18 If 24 cards are used
how many children can play?

19 How many 8s in 16?

20 How many 8s in 48?

21 How many 8s in 72?

22 How many 8s in 56?

23 How many 8s in 8?

24 How many 8s in 80?

1	2	3	4	5	6	7	8
9	10	11	12	13	14	15	16
17	18	19	20	21	22	23	24
25	26	27	28	29	30	31	32
33	34	35	36	37	38	39	40
41	42	43	44	45	46	47	48
49	50	51	52	53	54	55	56
57	58	59	60	61	62	63	64
65	66	67	68	69	70	71	72
73	74	75	76	77	78	79	80

Copy and finish the charts for this card game.

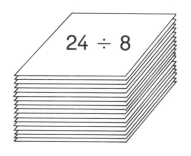

$24 \div 8$

25

$24 \div 8$

$8\overline{)64}$

$32 \div 8$

$8\overline{)56}$

$16 \div 8$

26

$40 \div 8$

$8\overline{)80}$

$8 \div 8$

$8\overline{)48}$

$72 \div 8$

27 13 cards are shared between two people.
They get 6 cards each.
1 card is left over.

$13 \div 2 = \square$ remainder $\square$ $\quad 2\overline{)13}$ $\square$ r $\square$

Share these cards between two people.

28 19 cards   **29** 15 cards   **30** 21 cards   **31** 17 cards

32 44 cards are shared between 3 children.
How many cards each? How many left?

33 $3\overline{)43}$ **34** $3\overline{)46}$ **35** $3\overline{)52}$ **36** $3\overline{)37}$

Let's investigate

Use any two cards at a time.
Make numbers that divide exactly by 7.
Make numbers that divide exactly by 8.

B Use cards to help you.

1 How many sets of 7 cards can be made from 23 cards?

2 How many cards left over?

3 How many sets of 8 cards can be made from 35 cards?

4 How many cards left over?

Do these.

5 $7\overline{)17}$ 6 $7\overline{)20}$ 7 $7\overline{)39}$ 8 $7\overline{)43}$

9 $8\overline{)20}$ 10 $8\overline{)39}$ 11 $8\overline{)42}$ 12 $8\overline{)67}$

13 $85 \div 7$ 14 $93 \div 7$ 15 $89 \div 8$ 16 $98 \div 8$

Let's investigate

Find numbers that give a remainder of 2
when you divide them by 7.

Keep dividing these numbers by 2 until you can't divide exactly by 2 again.

Try 20.

$20 \div 2 = 10 \qquad 10 \div 2 = 5$

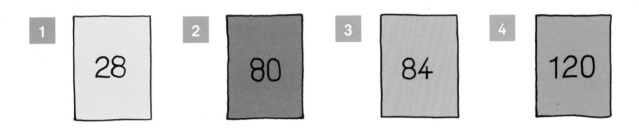

1 28   **2** 80   **3** 84   **4** 120

5 Find another number between 30 and 40 that will divide by 2 and reach an answer of 1.

Let's investigate

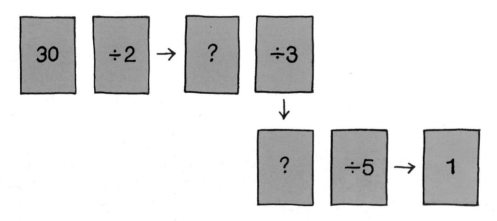

30    $\div 2 \rightarrow$? $\div 3$

? $\div 5 \rightarrow$ 1

Find other numbers that go exactly to 1 when you divide them three times.
You may choose the three numbers to divide them by.